Pebble Plus

EXTREME EARTH

HOTTEST PLACES
ON THE PLANET

by Karen Soll

raintree

a Capstone company — publishers for children

Raintree is an imprint of Capstone Global Library Limited, a company incorporated in England and Wales having its registered office at 264 Banbury Road, Oxford, OX2 7DY – Registered company number: 6695582

www.raintree.co.uk
myorders@raintree.co.uk

Editorial Credits
Karen Soll, editor; Juliette Peters, designer;
Tracy Cummins, media specialist; Tori Abraham, production specialist

ISBN 978 1 4747 1264 4
20 19 18 17 16 15
10 9 8 7 6 5 4 3 2 1

British Library Cataloguing in Publication Data
A full catalogue record for this book is available from the British Library.

Photo Credits
Alamy: Eric Chahi, 15, imageBROKER, 11, Kris Wiktor, 13; Getty Images: Tim Bewer, 9; NOAA: Dr. Bob Embley/NOAA PMEL, Chief Scientist, 19; Shutterstock: Aleksandra H. Kossowska, Cover Top Right, 3, Anton Prado, Design Element, 1, beboy, Cover Top Left, Galyna Andrushko, Cover Bottom, Ivsanmas, Map, Johan Swanepoel, 21, samarttiw, 7, 22-23, ssguy, 5; Thinkstock: Dorling Kindersley, 17

Every effort has been made to contact copyright holders of material reproduced in this book. Any omissions will be rectified in subsequent printings if notice is given to the publisher.

All the internet addresses (URLs) given in this book were valid at the time of going to press. However, due to the dynamic nature of the internet, some addresses may have changed, or sites may have changed or ceased to exist since publication. While the author and publisher regret any inconvenience this may cause readers, no responsibility for any such changes can be accepted by either the author or the publisher.

Note to Parents and Teachers

The Extreme Earth set supports topics related to earth science. This book describes and illustrates climate and geography. The images support early readers in understanding the text. The repetition of words and phrases helps early readers learn new words. This book also introduces early readers to subject-specific vocabulary, which is defined in the Glossary section. Early readers may need assistance to read some words and to use the Table of contents, Glossary, Read more, Websites, Critical thinking questions, and Index sections of the book.

Printed and bound in China.

CONTENTS

HOT PLACES

Think about being outside on a hot day. Some places are hotter than others. Let's find out which places get really hot!

Bangkok, Thailand, gets very hot.

The air is wet and heavy.

It feels hotter than it is.

The average daytime temperature in Bangkok is 32 degrees Celsius (90 degrees Fahrenheit).

One valley in Ethiopia is like
a bowl that traps heat.

It is very hot. Only a few people
have seen it.

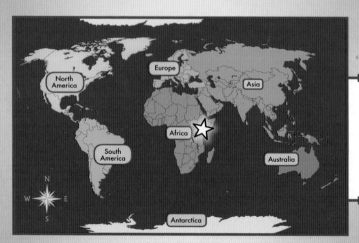

Dallol is a place that sits in the valley.
The temperature in Dallol never drops
below 34 degrees Celsius (93 degrees
Fahrenheit).

HOTTER PLACES

What if your town

was hot for 160 days?

Marble Bar has that record.

This desert town is in Australia.

From 31 October 1923, temperatures stayed above 38 degrees Celsius (100 degrees Fahrenheit) for 160 days.

Furnace Creek Ranch

is in California.

This hot place is in a desert

called Death Valley.

On 7 October 1913, the temperature on the ranch was 57 degrees Celsius (134 degrees Fahrenheit). This set a record for the hottest temperature in the western half of the world.

One place in the Sahara
had a very hot day. It was
the hottest day ever recorded.
This happened in 1922.

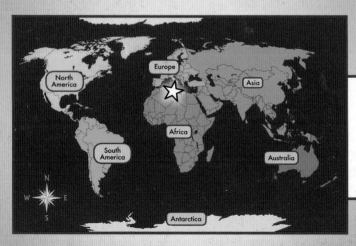

On 13 September 1922,
the temperature in Al Aziziyah,
Libya, was 58 degrees Celsius
(136 degrees Fahrenheit).

HOTTEST PLACES

Molten rock in Earth
gets very hot. Rocks above
it crack. Water gets into
these cracks.

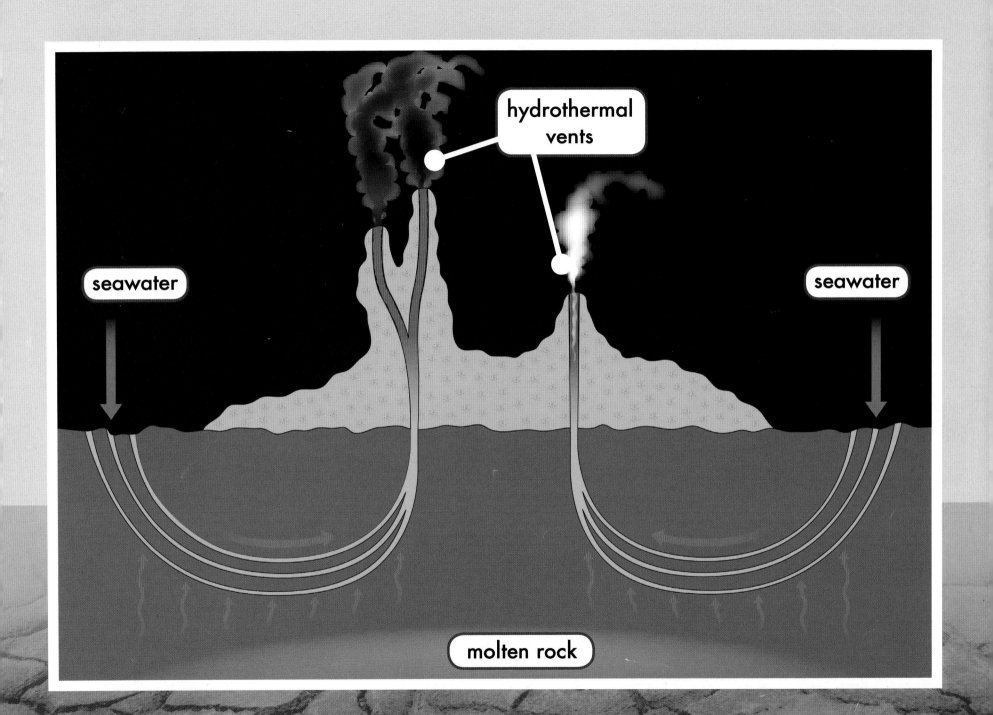

hydrothermal vents

seawater

seawater

molten rock

The water gets hot and bursts to the surface as steam. The steam is so hot it can melt lead.

The hottest spot is Earth's core.

You can't see Earth's core.

There are other hot spots you

can visit. Which place would you

like to see?

Earth's core has a
recorded temperature of
3,677 degrees Celsius
(6,650 degrees Fahrenheit).

core

GLOSSARY

core—the inner part of Earth that is made of metal, rocks and melted rock

desert—a dry area with little rain

melt—to change from a solid to a liquid because of heat

molten—melted by heat

recorded—written so it can be used or seen again in the future

steam—a hot gas from water that is heated

temperature—the measure of how hot or cold something is

valley—a low area of land between hills or mountains

READ MORE

Earth's Hottest Place and Other Earth Science Records (Wow!), Martha E. H. Rustad (Capstone Press, 2014)

Harsh Habitats (Extreme Nature), Anita Ganeri (Heinemann-Raintree, 2013)

Seymour Simon's Extreme Earth Records, Seymour Simon (Chronicle Books, 2012)

WEBSITES

http://www.neok12.com/Deserts.htm

Learn why certain places are called deserts, and watch videos or play games about these hot places.

http://kids.britannica.com/comptons/article-9276838/Sahara

Discover more about the world's largest desert.

http://www.nps.gov/deva/learn/kidsyouth/index.htm

What can you do in Death Valley? Find out by visiting this website.

CRITICAL THINKING QUESTIONS

1. How can a valley be like a bowl that traps heat?

2. How is Marble Bar like another desert in this book?

3. Draw a picture of how molten rock can cause steam.
   Label your picture.

INDEX

Year: 2